FEARSOME GIANTS

FANTASY CREATURES

Gareth Stevens PUBLISHING

HOT TOPICS

BY BENJAMIN PROUDFIT

Please visit our website, www.garethstevens.com. For a free color catalog of all our high-quality books, call toll free 1-800-542-2595 or fax 1-877-542-2596.

Library of Congress Cataloging-in-Publication Data
Names: Proudfit, Benjamin author
Title: Fearsome giants / Benjamin Proudfit.
Other titles: Giants
Description: Buffalo, NY : Gareth Stevens Publishing, [2026] | Series: Fantasy creatures | Includes index.
Identifiers: LCCN 2025019668 (print) | LCCN 2025019669 (ebook) | ISBN 9781482475227 (library binding) | ISBN 9781482475210 (paperback) | ISBN 9781482475234 (ebook)
Subjects: LCSH: Giants (Folklore)–Juvenile literature | Giants (Folklore) in literature | LCGFT: Literature.
Classification: LCC GR560 .P76 2026 (print) | LCC GR560 (ebook) | DDC 398.21–dc23/eng/20250702
LC record available at https://lccn.loc.gov/2025019668
LC ebook record available at https://lccn.loc.gov/2025019669

Published in 2026 by
Gareth Stevens Publishing
2544 Clinton Street
Buffalo, NY 14224

Designer: Leslie Taylor
Editor: Kristen Nelson

Photo credits: Cover (giant) Shutterstock AI Generator/Shutterstock.com; cover and series art (neon circle) Ikrill/Shutterstock.com, (rough frame) TarnishArt/Shutterstock.com, (splotchy background) TiffanyShanks/Shutterstock.com; p. 5, 7, 9, 13, 17, 19, 25 Shutterstock AI Generator/Shuttertock.com; p. 11 (Fenrir) Mabel Dorothy Hardy (1868–1937)/File:Fenrir binded.png_commons.wikimedia.org; p. 14 Variopinta/Shutterstock.com; p. 17 P Maxwell Photography/Shutterstock.com; p. 21 jvoves/Flickr.com; p. 23 Ovidiu Hrubaru/Shutterstock.com; p. 27 Toho Company Ltd./File:Godzilla (1954).jpg_commons.wikimedia.org; p. 29 fotopanorama360/Shutterstock.com; p. 30 (squid) Arip Apandi/Shutterstock.com; (whale) Ajit S N/Shutterstock.com, (crocodile) Alizada Studios/Shutterstock.com, (anaconda) Patrick K. Campbell/Shutterstock.com.

Printed in China

CPSIA compliance information: Batch #QWGS26: For further information contact Gareth Stevens, at 1-800-542-2595.

CONTENTS

Meet the Giants

People have been telling stories about **fantastic** creatures for centuries. Giants appear in **mythology** around the world. These supersized, humanlike creatures were commonly mean and not very smart. Today, giants still come up in **fantasy** stories—though many are kind!

IMAGINE THAT!

THERE'S NO SET SIZE FOR GIANTS IN STORIES. SOME TALES HAVE GIANTS THAT ARE SIMPLY LARGER THAN ADULT MEN. OTHERS TELL OF CREATURES AS LARGE AS HOUSES OR BIGGER!

Why Tell the Tale?

Myths are different from place to place. But why myths are passed down is the same for everyone. Myths allow a group of people to explain something that happens in the world around them. Myths teach lessons and give hope for the days to come.

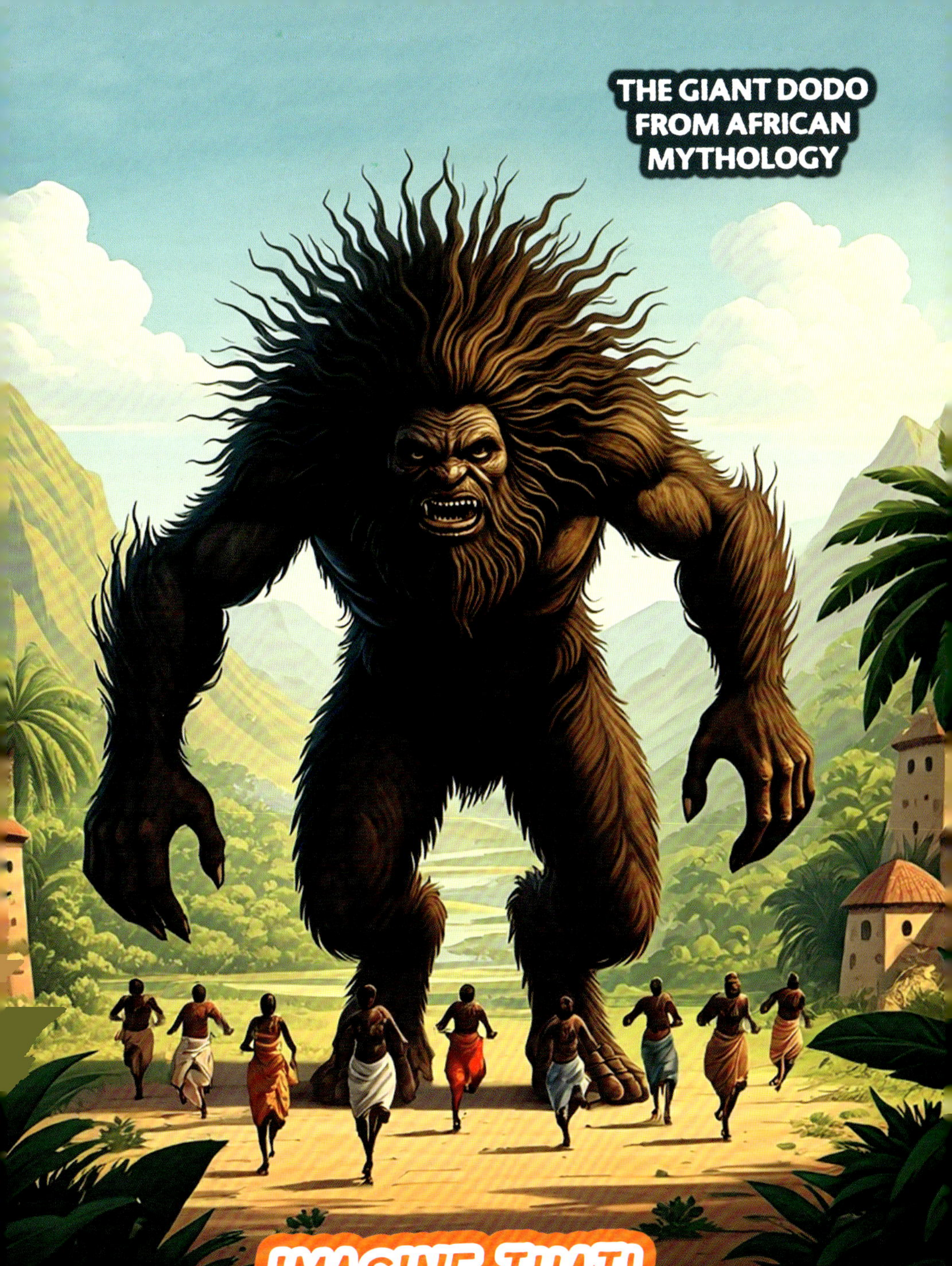

THE GIANT DODO FROM AFRICAN MYTHOLOGY

IMAGINE THAT!

MYTHS OFTEN TELL HOW THE WORLD AND HUMANS WERE CREATED, OR MADE.

Aurgelmir

In **Norse** mythology, the first living being is Aurgelmir (also called Ymir). He was a giant! He made all the giants of Norse stories. When Aurgelmir was killed, his body became Earth, which the Norse called Midgard.

IMAGINE THAT!

GIANTS IN NORSE MYTHOLOGY ARE CALLED JÖTUNN.

After this, the first Norse gods made a place for giants to live. It was cold and unwelcoming. Because of this, some giants that lived there were called frost giants. Norse myths also feature sea giants, fire giants, and giants that could take the form of animals.

IMAGINE THAT!

FENRIR IS ONE GIANT THAT APPEARS AS A HUGE WOLF IN NORSE MYTHOLOGY.

FENRIR

One-Eyed Giants

Ancient Greek myths tell of a whole race of giants called Gigantes. They were the children of one of the first beings in Greek mythology, Gaia. Huge and scary to look at, these giants fought the gods, such as Zeus.

IMAGINE THAT!

ZEUS WAS THE KING OF THE GREEK GODS.

ZEUS

Other Greek myths feature Cyclopes. These giants only had one eye and ate people! The most well-known Cyclopes story today comes from the *Odyssey*. It features the hero Odysseus **blinding** a Cyclops named Polyphemus.

IMAGINE THAT!

THE *ODYSSEY* WAS WRITTEN AROUND 700 BCE. IT TELLS OF OTHER FANTASTIC CREATURES SUCH AS THE MINOTAUR. IT HAD THE HEAD AND TAIL OF A BULL AND THE BODY OF A MAN.

ODYSSEUS BLINDING POLYPHEMUS

Goliath, Felled

The Bible has a giant in it too! It tells of a battle in which a young shepherd, David, takes on a giant named Goliath. David uses a slingshot and stone to hit Goliath between the eyes. Goliath falls!

IMAGINE THAT!

TODAY, A "FIGHT BETWEEN DAVID AND GOLIATH" MEANS ONE SIDE IS STRONGER THAN THE OTHER. THE WEAKER SIDE WILL NEED TO FIGURE OUT A CLEVER WAY TO WIN.

SLINGSHOT

Asian Myths

Giants are also found in the myths of Asia. One Chinese myth tells of Pan Gu, the being that created Earth. For thousands of years, he had to hold heaven and Earth apart. He grew taller and taller as he pushed up the sky.

IMAGINE THAT!

IN THE MYTH, PAN GU HATCHES, OR COMES OUT OF, A SPECIAL EGG!

Jack's Giant

Do you know the story of "Jack and the Beanstalk"? A boy grows a beanstalk with magic beans. He climbs it to a giant's castle in the sky. The giant can smell Jack and wants to use his bones to make bread!

IMAGINE THAT!

THE STORY OF JACK AND THE MAGIC BEANSTALK IS A EUROPEAN FAIRY TALE THAT'S BEEN AROUND FOR HUNDREDS OF YEARS.

Big Bunyan

Paul Bunyan is a giant man from North American **folktales**. The many stories about him say that as a child he was stronger than many men. It was often said he was 7 feet (2.1 m) tall. Tales also say Bunyan had a giant blue ox named Babe!

IMAGINE THAT!

STORIES OF PAUL BUNYAN SAY HE WAS SO BIG AND STRONG, HE COULD BRING DOWN A WHOLE FOREST WITH ONE CHOP OF HIS AX!

STATUE OF
PAUL BUNYAN AND BLUE IN
KLAMATH, CALIFORNIA

Giants Today

Even today, giants play a part in fantasy books and movies. The Roald Dahl book *The BFG* features a friendly giant. Rubeus Hagrid, from the *Harry Potter* series, is a half-giant. The Earth Giants in *Frozen II* are taller than the trees—and get mad when they're woken from sleep!

IMAGINE THAT!

IN THE BOOK *HARRY POTTER AND THE SORCERER'S STONE*, HAGRID IS SAID TO BE TWICE THE HEIGHT OF A MAN AND FIVE TIMES AS WIDE!

Giants like Hagrid are good guys! But many movies use giants as the **villain**. King Kong and Godzilla are giant monsters that can destroy cities. Often, something evil is made giant to make it even worse. Think about Ursula in *The Little Mermaid* growing to impossible size!

IMAGINE THAT!

THE GIANT GODZILLA WAS FIRST SEEN ON THE BIG SCREEN IN 1954'S *GODZILLA*.

GODZILLA

Fact or Fiction?

Do you think giants could have been real? With so many stories about them, it might seem possible that they once walked Earth. However, human giants have never existed, or lived. In fact, ancient humans were probably shorter than modern humans!

IMAGINE THAT!

THE TALLEST PERSON EVER MEASURED WAS ROBERT WADLOW. HE STOOD 8 FEET 11 INCHES (2.7 M) TALL!

ROBERT
WADLOW

Real-Life Giants

GIANT SQUID

weight: up to 2,000 pounds (907 kg)

length: up to 45 feet (14 m)

BLUE WHALE

weight: more than 330,000 pounds (150,000 kg)

length: about 110 feet (34 m)

SALTWATER CROCODILE

weight: up to 2,200 pounds (1,000 kg)

length: 23 feet (7 m)

GREEN ANACONDA

weight: 550 pounds (250 kg)

length: 30 feet (9.1 m)

FOR MORE INFORMATION

BOOKS

Munsey, Lizzie, et al. *Supernatural Creatures: Mythical and Sacred Creatures from Around the World.* New York, NY: DK, 2024.

Nardo, Don. *Creatures and Beasts in World Mythology.* San Diego, CA: ReferencePoint Press, Inc., 2025.

WEBSITES

Giants in Greek Mythology
https://www.theoi.com/greek-mythology/giants.html
Read about more giants from ancient Greece.

Have Giant Humans Ever Existed?
https://www.livescience.com/archaeology/have-giant-humans-ever-existed
Do you think giants were ever real? Check out the facts in this article.

Publisher's note to educators and parents: Our editors have carefully reviewed these websites to ensure that they are suitable for students. Many websites change frequently, however, and we cannot guarantee that a site's future contents will continue to meet our high standards of quality and educational value. Be advised that students should be closely supervised whenever they access the internet.

GLOSSARY

ancient: From long ago.

blind: To make unable to see.

fantastic: Not real.

fantasy: Having to do with imaginative stories that feature impossible events and characters.

folktale: A story passed down by people over time.

mythology: All of the stories told by a people to explain practices, beliefs, and natural events.

Norse: Having to do with ancient Norway.

villain: A person who does bad things.

INDEX